Philosophy for children

From child to children

Once upon a time!

Egg carton!

Coloring story!

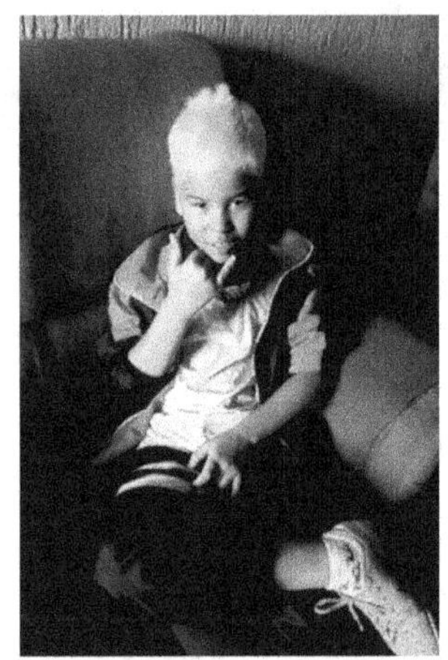

By: Bernardo Octaviano Pereira

This book
belongs to:

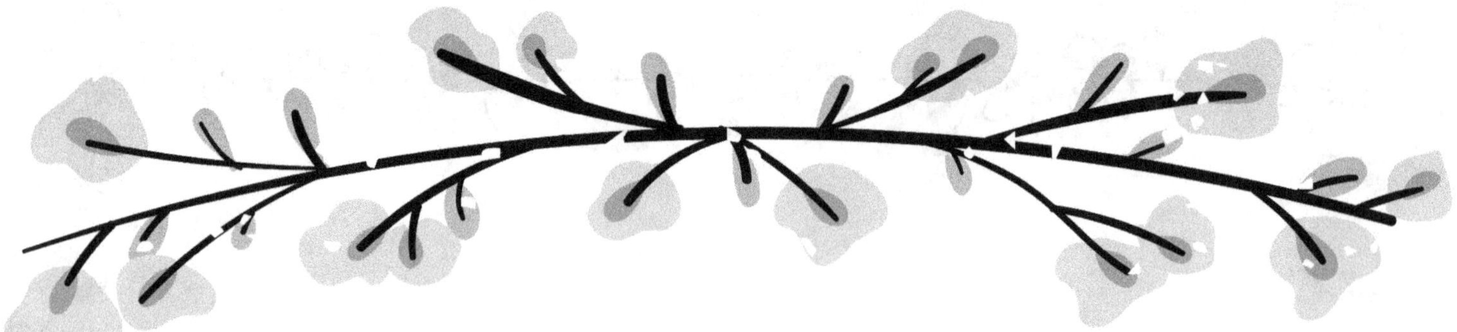

I dedicate this work, firstly, to my parents who I love so much, to my teachers, to my dear aunts and to all my friends, may God bless you all infinitely!

Bernardo Octaviano Pereira

16/04/2024

Once upon a time, in a neighborhood away from the city, a lively party celebrated the joy of life. At the end of the party,

When everyone was getting ready to leave, an elderly woman accompanied by her granddaughter asked some young people for a ride.

She explained that they needed to get to a closer bus stop and said that they always had the company of "daddy in heaven" on their journeys.

The driver, laughing and joking, suggested that there was only room in the trunk of the car for her, the girl and "daddy in heaven".

Everyone, still excited and a little drunk, got into the car and drove off, screeching tires and laughing loudly along the road.

Shortly afterwards, the lady got a ride with a couple who were also leaving the party. Together, they headed down the dark, winding road. However, in a nearby stretch,

They came across a terrible scene: the young people's car, which had initially denied them a ride, was completely destroyed, lying on a cliff.

Horror gripped everyone as they saw the devastation in front of them. Rescuers quickly arrived at the scene of the accident. However, amidst the wreckage,

In the trunk something surprising remained intact: a carton of eggs. It was as if the "daddy in heaven" was there, protecting them even in the midst of tragedy.

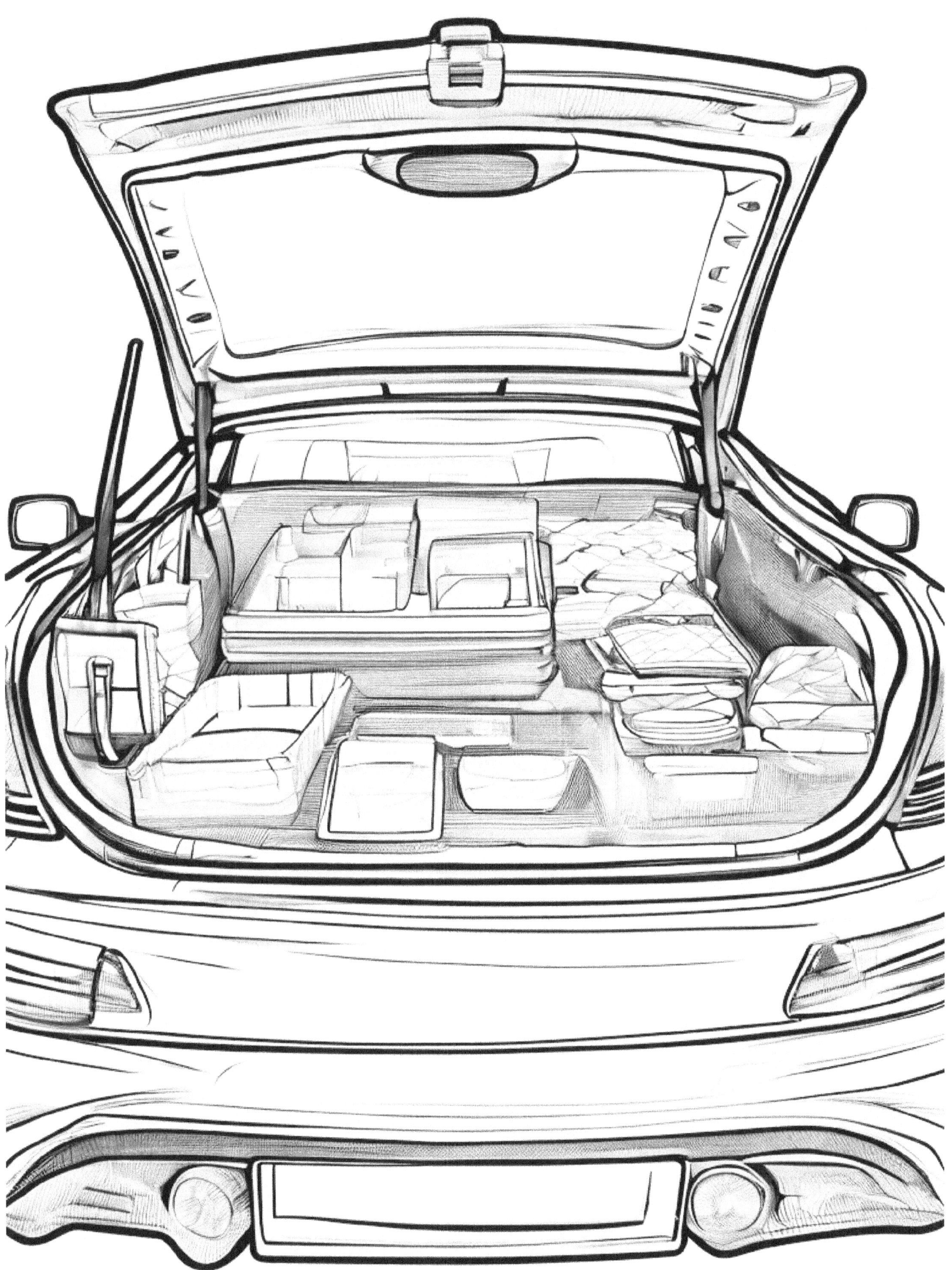

This experience left a deep mark on survivors and the community. The lady, with tears in her eyes, thanked the "daddy in heaven"

for his miraculous protection. They understood that sometimes safety and security come from where we least expect it, in the most unexpected moments.

This story reminds us of the importance of walking with faith and gratitude in our hearts, trusting that, even in the darkest moments,

"Heavenly Father" is always with us, protecting us and guiding us on our journey through life, always walk with "Heavenly Father"!

The end!